ECCLESIASTES/SONG OF SOLOMON

SOLOMON

Daily Devotionals Volume 13

TABLE OF CONTENTS

HISTORY REPEATED

Eccl. 1:9-11 History merely repeats itself; it has all been done before. Nothing under the sun is truly new. What can you point to that is new? How do you know it didn't already exist long ago? We don't remember what happened in those former times. And in future generations, no one will remember what we are doing now.

We are merely reliving the past. The way we live may be different than previous generations, but in essence, nothing has changed. We face the same battles that have been fought for generations and generations. There is a constant spiritual warfare that has plagued humanity since sin was first introduced on earth. All people make choices daily in who they will serve, God or Satan. Sometimes we win battles and sometimes we lose them. It will continue to be that way until Jesus comes to send Satan into the depths of hell for eternity.

Life is lived in the moment. Not every

moment of life is recorded to refer to. Be assured, over the course of history, whatever you are going through in life has already been lived. Your life is no different from anyone else's. Others have fought and won your battles and you can too. History is full of a great cloud of witnesses that there is victory over your struggles. Satan wants you to believe that no one understands your struggles but you. He wants you to buckle underneath the load and not have any hope that there is a way out. He wants you to give up and not persevere until victory is found.

No one may remember you in future generations, but you can leave a great legacy for those who know you if you don't cave in. You can show them that in Christ, all things are possible. You can show them that the Lord does not abandon His children. You can show them that there is indeed hope for them to in Jesus. How you live today may affect the lives of many for years to come. Stay strong in faith and let the Lord lead you step by step to the victory that is yours in Him.   2

THE DEPRAVITY OF MAN

Eccl. 1:9-11 History merely repeats itself; it has all been done before. Nothing under the sun is truly new. What can you point to that is new? How do you know it didn't already exist long ago? We don't remember what happened in those former times. And in future generations, no one will remember what we are doing now.

Things never change. The details may vary, but the things that are happening today are merely a repeat of what has happened before. Man's nature is today what it was the day Adam and Eve disobeyed God and ushered in sin into the world. It has reared its ugly head in unimaginable ways, and it always will. Without Christ changing it, the heart remains desperately wicked.

You cannot read history without being exposed to the ugliness and destructive nature of sin. It is the cause of all the inhumane treatment that has plagued humanity. It is the cause of all the hatred amongst men. It is the cause of all the self-serving throughout history. We don't have to live in the past to know that it is true. Secular and Biblical history are all the proof we need. As much as we would like to convince ourselves, there never has been an age of innocence since the time of the fall of man.

All the atrocities that have plagued man throughout history are not recorded. Because of the advent of modern technology we have been exposed to some of the worst of what man can do to man, but we cannot say that it hasn't been done before. The sin encrusted soul is capable of any form of evil that you could ever imagine. It will continue to be the way it us for as long as man is on the earth. As bad as things are and has been, we know that the worst is yet to come.

God has warned us of what to expect on earth after Jesus comes and takes the church out of it. Unimaginable horror will plague the earth. When God removes His hand of protection over the earth, evil will rule unbridled. It will be a time in which not only will man suffer from one another, but God will unleash the horrors of nature upon man as a result of his sins.

The future may be bleak, but you don't have to be a victim of it. God gives us a way of escape, and it is Christ Jesus our Lord. God promises us a bright and glorious future if we put our trust and confidence in Him. We have nothing to fear when Jesus is our Savior and Lord. We can boldly face the future with our lives rooted and established in Christ. Is Jesus your Savior today?

LIFE MEANING

Eccl. 2:10-11 Anything I wanted, I took. I did not restrain myself from any joy. I even found great pleasure in hard work, an additional reward for all my labors. But as I looked at everything I had worked so hard to accomplish, it was all so meaningless. It was like chasing the wind. There was nothing really worthwhile anywhere.

What are you living for? What gives your life meaning? We spend our entire lives trying to give our lives meaning. Most will try to do good things. Many try to carve their niche out in the world. Many will seek fame, fortune or a following. Many put all their energy in their families. Many will rally around a cause they are passionate about. Many are working hard for the day in which they can retire and coast the rest of the days of their lives.

No matter what you are working for to give your life meaning, it is all meaningless if what you are living for is rooted in the world. There is nothing on earth that really give life meaning. We live and then die. Whatever we live for dies with us. We can't take anything on earth with us when we die. It is all so meaningless, a chasing after the wind.

It is only when we find our meaning in relationship with Christ that we find something worth living for. Nothing on earth can promise us eternal life. Nothing can do us any good as far as keeping us out of hell. Our only hope of eternal life is to live life in Christ. Only Christ can assure us that what we are doing makes any difference at all.

Dear friend, take a careful and honest look at your life. What are you relying on to give your life meaning? If it is not a relationship with Christ, you are living in vain. You may be enjoying the fruit of your labors now, but it won't last. Your purpose for life will die with you if you do not have Christ. If you know Christ, live like it. Put your heart into it. Make the Lord your number one priority in your life. It is only in Christ that you will find a hope that will not die.

If you don't know that Christ is your Savior, today is the day you must get right with God. You don't know if you will see the end of your day. Your life will take on a whole new meaning if you will let Him into your heart. You will find that there is indeed something worth living for. Christ will forgive you of your sins if you turn to Him, confess them, repent, and ask Him for forgiveness. What are you waiting for? Do it now. You will be glad you did.

ENJOYING LIFE

Eccl. 3:9-14 What do people really get for all their hard work? I have thought about this in connection with the various kinds of work God has given people to do. God has made everything beautiful for its own time. He has planted eternity in the human heart, but even so, people cannot see the whole scope of God's work from beginning to end. So I concluded that there is nothing better for people than to be happy and to enjoy themselves as long as they can. And people should eat and drink and enjoy the fruits of their labor; for these are gifts from God.

In other words, enjoy what you are doing in life. Not every job is enjoyable, but you can find a way to enjoy it. How? Learn first how to enjoy life. If you have a positive outlook on yourself and the life you live, whatever work you have to do will be far less painful and far more enjoyable. Do you enjoy this journey of life? Do you have a sense of your purpose for living? Do you have hope for your future?

The ability to enjoy living is directly connected to your relationship with Christ. Jesus puts meaning to the bones of life. He not only impacts our future, he impacts our present. He gives us a reason to enjoy life, no matter the circumstances we are in. We find purpose and meaning in Him. He gives us something worthwhile to live for. He gives us hope. And knowing all that He has done, is doing now, and what He is yet going to do for us, enables us to enjoy the process of living. In Christ we know that we are better off than we have ever been and we shall be far better off than we are now.

Enjoy your life. Enjoy all that the Lord gives you to do. Enjoy the fruits of your labors. Life is a gift from God and is meant to be enjoyed. Jesus came to give us life and not just life, but life more abundantly. The closer you live to Christ, the more enjoyable your life will be.

OUR SIN PROBLEM

Eccl. 3: 18 Then I realized that God allows people to continue in their sinful ways so he can test them. That way, they can see for themselves that they are no better than animals.

If God wanted to, He could make us do what is right in His eyes. He could force His ways upon us. He could take care of sin without any problem at all. But, He has not chosen to do it. In a lot of ways, I think it would make living a much easier process. At least then, we wouldn't be constantly struggling to not sin. But then, we would be merely robots in God's hands and not able to have a love relationship with Him. We would not be able to know Him in a deep and personal way, as one who helps us in our times of need and struggles.

God knows that the real test of one's faith is how we handle sin. He knows what we should know, that if we are His children we will not continue to sin against Him.

11

God is holy and there is no sin found in Him. If He lives in us and controls us, then we should not sin against Him. It's as simple and plain as that. There is no wiggle room when it comes to sin. It is detestable to God and will be judged by Him.

No one has to tell you that sin is a problem for you. We all know that we are not as godly as we would like to be or as others perceive us to be. Sin is common to all people. The more sin we see in us, the more we realize that we need the Lord. We must have the Lord's help if we are going to have victory over sin, because it is too powerful for us to overcome on our own.

When we don't let the Lord help us, we will do as the animals do; we will follow our sinful instincts. We can't change our ways on our own. We are born sinners and will die sinners without the Lord. Denying that it is so does not change it. God makes it very clear in His Word.

You will never know the peace of God

while dabbling in sin. You will know how strong your faith really is by how well you resist sinning. Your love for God is seen in how you handle sin. If you find yourself yielding to sin more than you do resisting it, you are not living in fellowship with God.

Dear friend. Only Jesus can help you with your sin problem. No one can stop you from sinning, but Christ can help you overcome your desire to sin. Let Jesus be your Lord and you will discover that you will no longer be a victim to sin; instead, you will be a victor over it.

HAPPY WHILE YOU WORK

Eccl. 3:22-23 So I saw that there is nothing better for people than to be happy in their work. That is why they are here! No one will bring them back from death to enjoy life in the future.

What do you do for work? Are you happy in it? Why, or why not? Most people are not happy with their jobs. They feel stuck because they would much rather be doing something else with their life. They may have taken a particular job out of necessity and have just settled into it as a way of earning a living. We rationalize things and find all kinds of reasons why we should be doing something different. We may see ourselves as being too good or too qualified for what we do. We may think we deserve better pay for what we do. We may not get along well with our co-workers. On and on our rationalizations go. But, I believe that for most of us our dissatisfaction with what we do is more of a spiritual issue than it is anything else.

If you are not happy with yourself or are not right with God, no matter what your work may be, you will struggle and not be happy. Happiness stems from an attitude of gratitude to God. It is being God-centered and Christ-focused. It is knowing that we owe our all to God. True happiness is understanding that all of life is a gift and a blessing from God. It is giving to God the credit He deserves for who we are, what we are, and what we do. True happiness is never found outside of a life that is not Christ-centered.

When we live life in Christ, we do what we do to honor and glorify Him and not ourselves. We work at what we do with our best efforts. We strive to be a pleasing aroma unto God. We see our work as a part of our witness. Sure work can be mundane and cumbersome. We may not particularly like what we do, but, if we approach it as a gift from God and an opportunity to serve Him, work ceases to be burdensome.

If you are struggling to find happiness

in your work, first seek your happiness in Christ. Learn to love Him with all your heart, mind and soul. Learn how to walk with Him wherever you go. Learn how to let Him be the delight of your heart from morning to night. Let Him be Lord of your heart and your heart will sing His praises no matter what you may do in life. Let your life work be a living testimony of your love for the Lord. When your heart is right with the Lord, you will be able to give Him praise and thanksgiving in and for all things, even in your work.

ENVYING OTHERS

Eccl. 4:4 Then I observed that most people are motivated to success by their envy of their neighbors. But this, too, is meaningless, like chasing the wind.

Do you envy others? Where is it getting you? Think about it. If you are motivated to do whatever you can do to get ahead because others are more successful than you, you are probably a mess. No matter how hard you try, you will find yourself always falling behind what others are doing. Comparing yourself to others is always a losing game. You will not be satisfied because you are not as successful as others, and you will become proud because you are better than others.

Success is a relative thing. We all measure success in different ways. The only success that will satisfy the soul is living right with God. It is enough to simply know that God is with us, living in us, working in us, and working through us. Everything else is meaningless in life. The sooner we understand this truth, the better chance we have of being successful in life.

What is it going to really matter when you are dying what you have accomplished in this world? What will help you to die in peace? Will you really care then how big your bank account is or how many possessions you own? Will it really matter how much influence you have on others? Will your lifework matter to you? When you know you are breathing your last few breaths of life, nothing will matter to you, except perhaps your thoughts about what is next.

What will matter when we are on the threshold of death is where we will spend eternity. We will want to know that we will be in heaven and not hell. Very few people will be in total denial that there is an eternity awaiting them. The sad thing is that most want to wait until they know that they are dying before they take eternity seriously. They live in denial that death is unpredictable. No one knows when they will die. Waiting for that unknown and unpredictable day is foolishness. Death is but one breath away for all of us.

Don't mess around and wait to be ready to die. Live each moment in Christ and you will not be caught off guard. Don't take the opportunity the Lord is giving you to live rightly with Him lightly or for granted. If you die today without Christ as your Savior, you will spend eternity in hell.

TEAMWORK

Eccl. 4:9-10 Two people can accomplish more than twice as much as one; they get a better return for their labor. If one person falls, the other can reach out and help. But people who are alone when they fall are in real trouble.

I worked in a factory for many years where sometimes I worked alone and at other times I had a partner. I normally was able to get a lot more done working with someone than I did by working alone. Having a partner enabled me to focus on doing well specific tasks rather than trying to do more tasks and not do them as well. When two people work together well, much more can be accomplished than one can do by himself.

Working together enables each worker to help the other when they need it. It encourages each worker to know they are not alone, that someone is always there to help get the job done. The same thing holds true in our spiritual lives. We need to live in partnership with both the Lord and others. When we try to do things on our own, there is no one to help us when we run into trouble.

When we begin to think that we have things under control and start to neglect our relationship with Christ, we soon find ourselves in trouble with God. We let down our guard and sinful attitudes and behavior soon creep in. We begin to not read our Bibles and prayer takes a back seat in our lives. No one can neglect the Lord and make it spiritually. Our greatest need in life is the Lord. We are partners with Him in faith. We will always accomplish more with the Lord in it than we will without Him.

It is also true regarding other believers. We need others in our lives who can help us in our walk of faith and the working out of our faith in the world. Much more will be accomplished for the Lord when we are working in partnership with others. We feed off of others and grow more when we live in relationship with them. There simply is no room for loners in our faith walk.

Don't get yourself in trouble with the Lord. Surround yourself with His grace and holiness and the fellowship of others. We simply cannot do it alone, no matter how gifted we may be or how well equipped we may be.

STRENGTH IN NUMBERS

Eccl. 4:12-13 A person standing alone can be attacked and defeated, but two can stand back-to-back and conquer. Three are even better, for a triple-braided cord is not easily broken.

There is strength in numbers. By ourselves we are too weak to stand for long. The opposition is too great and strong. We are easily overwhelmed. It is true both physically and spiritually.

No one is so strong spiritually that he can withstand Satan for long on his own. We need others in our lives who understand what we are going through and who can support us in our struggles. We need wisdom and guidance beyond ourselves because often we simply do not know what to do. When someone is standing by our side, we feel stronger and more confident in our struggles. We do not feel all alone and are not as likely to give up and admit defeat.

It is better still when not only are there

others standing with us to support us, but we have the Lord on our side. Quite frankly, unless the Lord is the third strand that binds the cord together, we will not overcome Satan. Two strands woven together are stronger than one and can withstand a lot, but three strands are much stronger and not easily defeated. No matter how good our intentions may be, without the Lord, we will not prevail.

Satan attacks us on many different fronts. When we shore up our defenses in one area, he attacks another. No matter how well protected we may be, we will always be vulnerable outside of the Lord's protection. When people are united together by Christ, the gates of hell itself shall not prevail against them. People may be able to do much good and make a huge difference in the world working together, but without the Lord in it Satan will easily render the good useless.

In the church, in marriage, in the workplace, in all we do, we need the Lord to bind us together. It is impossible to please God without Christ. All of our labors are in vain without the Lord. Life lived out without the help and blessings of Christ is futile. He alone holds us all together. He is the head of the Church and we are His body. He is the Lord of life and the sooner we let Him be, the better we will be able to live in victory and not defeat.

SILENT WORSHIP

Eccl. 5:1-2 As you enter the house of God, keep your ears open and your mouth shut! Don't be a fool who doesn't realize that mindless offerings to God are evil. And don't make rash promises to God, for he is in heaven and you are only here on earth. So, let your words be few.

Wow. How many of us are in churches where silence is a good thing? It seems like the church today is more about noise and busyness than it is silence and meditation. We have gotten to the point where we are uncomfortable in the quiet. We surround ourselves with noise and chatter so much that we just don't know how to wait patiently before God anymore. Yes, there are churches that practice silence where the soul can reflect on her standing before God. But, it is not the practice of most churches.

We are reminded in today's verses that it is better to be quiet and listen than it is to always be talking. All of us think we have profound things to say, but do we really need to say them? Why is it that we don't keep our mouths shut more than we do? We are not learning anything if we are talking. We won't hear what God is saying unless we are listening and not talking. Sure, there are times in which we add valuable insights to what is being taught, but we benefit more from listening and learning than we do by talking all the time.

When we are in the presence of God, it is important that we don't talk too much and make Him promises that we can't, or won't keep. We sometimes say things in the emotions of the moment that we later realize were rash and we live to regret it. It is foolish to make promises to God that we don't keep. God holds us accountable for the things we promise to Him.

We wonder why it is that we don't hear from God like we should. We wonder why it is that there seems to be little real sense of God's presence in our worship services. Could it be that it's because we have forgotten what it is like to be still and know that the Lord, He is God? They that wait on the Lord shall be renewed in their souls and receive strength for their journey of life.

Whether it is in public or private worship, put yourself in a position where you can hear from God and you will.

MEAN WHAT YOU SAY

Eccl. 5:1-2 As you enter the house of God, keep your ears open and your mouth shut! Don't be a fool who doesn't realize that mindless offerings to God are evil. And don't make rash promises to God, for he is in heaven, and you are only here on earth. So let your words be few.

I don't know about you, but these words really jump out at me. When was the last time you went to a church where no one was talking and moving about? How many of us go to church and sit still to meditate and prepare our hearts for worship? How many of us go to listen and learn? Could it be that we miss out on what God has to say because we are too distracted by our approach to worship that we can't hear him speak? Perhaps we need to rethink what the purpose of worship is. Could we benefit from more quiet and reflective time in our worship experiences?

How often do you carefully consider what you promise to God before you promise it? Do you make promises based on your emotions or careful thought? It is so easy to get caught up into the moment and react without considering what you are really doing. God does not take likely our commitments to Him. He keeps His word to us and expects us to do the same to Him. When you are moved to make a promise to God, wait before you do it. Give careful thought to your words because God will hold you accountable for them.

PREPARATION FOR WORSHIP

Eccl. 5:1-2 As you enter the house of God, keep your ears open and your mouth shut! Don't be a fool who doesn't realize that mindless offerings to God are evil. And don't make rash promises to God, for he is in heaven and you are only here on earth. So, let your words be few.

Are today's verses typical of your worship experience? Do you listen much and talk little or do you do like most people and socialize more than you meditate before your church service? I have been in a lot of church services over the years, and the typical scene is that people are talking right up to the moment the service is to begin. Time is spent connecting with others rather than with God.

Think about it for a moment. We best prepare ourselves for worship by quieting our hearts before God. It is when we focus on Him that we best worship Him. We experience the blessing of being in God's presence when we enter into His space. He is not found in the noise and clamor of the world around us; He is found in the stillness of our souls before Him.

The Lord is not another item on our agenda as we gather for worship; He is our agenda. He deserves our full attention. We can't switch gears from socializing one moment and focusing on the Lord the next. We need to spend some time in quiet before we approach Him in worship.

Also, we must do a better job of respecting who our Lord is, He is holy. We must understand that the Lord is who He is and act accordingly. Mindless offerings are what we bring to Him out of duty instead of love. Whatever it is we give or do before Him, if our hearts are not rightly connected to Him, it's all for nothing.

We must watch what we promise the Lord. If you don't mean what you say, don't say it. God judges the integrity of the heart. Say what you mean and mean what you say to the Lord. If you vow to do things differently in your life, then work hard to do it. Don't neglect your promises to God, for He holds you accountable for them.

EMPTY PROMISES

Eccl. 5:4-5 So when you make a promise to God, don't delay in following through, for God takes no pleasure in fools. Keep all the promises you make to him. It is better to say nothing than to promise something that you don't follow through on.

Much has already been said about the promises that we make to the Lord. There are two points in today's verses that we need to always strive to do. We must not put off what we promise to the Lord. We must get to work right away on keeping our word to Him. Take a moment and think about some of the promises you have made to the Lord. Did you promise to stop doing a particular sinful behavior? Did you promise to be more faithful in your personal devotions? Did you promise to pray for someone? Did you promise to give the Lord more of your time or resources? Did you promise to change your attitude or behavior towards someone? Did you promise to witness to someone? Whatever your promise may be, isn't it about time you did something about it? The Lord does hold us accountable for what we promise to Him.

It is much better to not promise the Lord anything than to promise something you can't or won't do. Think carefully about what you promise and do everything you can to act on it at once. If you need to write it down somewhere as a reminder, then do it. Don't be foolish and say things to the Lord without giving thought to them. He judges the integrity of the heart and will hold you responsible for keeping your word to Him.

KEEP YOUR PROMISES

Eccl. 5:4-6a So when you make a promise to God, don't delay in following through, for God takes no pleasure in fools. Keep all the promises you make to him. It is better to say nothing than to promise something that you don't follow through on. In such cases, your mouth is causing you to sin.

We need to take what we say to God seriously. Many make promises to God they never keep. There may be times of great stress and difficulty and you may promise God that if He would get you out of the mess you are in that you would devote yourself to Him in ways you never have before. You may promise Him full reign of your heart. You may promise Him your devoted service. We make all kind of promises to God, but they are meaningless if we don't keep them. In fact, they are much more than broken promises; God declares them to be sin.

What kind of promises have you made

to God? Have you kept them? Take a
moment and ask the Lord to remind you of
the promises you have made to Him. Maybe
you have forgotten all about them over time,
but if you ask Him to, the Lord will remind
you of them. God commands you to keep
your word to Him. If your situation has
changed and it is no longer feasible or
possible to keep your promise, ask the Lord
to forgive you and help you to not make
promises you won't keep from now on.

Why would we expect God to keep His
promises to us if we don't keep our promises
to Him? A person who loves someone does
not make empty promises. God commands
truthfulness from His children and we are
not being truthful if we make empty
promises to Him.

It is far better to keep silent and not say
anything at all to the Lord than it is to make
promises you don't keep. Don't sin against
the Lord by not keeping your word to Him.
If you need to ask the Lord to put a zip on
your lip, do it. Eternity is a long time to

think about the empty promises you have made to Him and not kept.

NEVER ENOUGH MONEY

Eccl. 5:10-11 Those who love money will never have enough. How absurd to think that wealth brings true happiness! The more you have, the more people come to help you spend it. So what is the advantage of wealth—except perhaps to watch it run through your fingers!

Those who love money have a lot more problems than they ever imagined. The love of money is insatiable. There is no end to the want for more. It drives a person to do things that they otherwise may not do in order to get more. It breeds selfishness. It hinders a person from getting close to God. It keeps people from getting close to other people. It causes a person to take advantage of others for personal gain. Money takes on such prominence in one's life that nothing else really matters. Those obsessed with money find they can't really trust anyone like they should and need to.

In addition to money becoming a driving force in one's life, it deceives one into thinking that there is a magical amount that once obtained will make a person happy. It is absurd to think that anything but God can make one happy.

Also, the more money a person has, the more people there will be to come alongside of you to help you spend it. People come out of the woodwork when they discover you have money. Our world is very adept at promoting ways for us to spend whatever money we have. People everywhere make all kinds of promises about how they can help make your life better if you give them money. People take advantage of people with wealth all the time. The allurement of being able to make more money by giving away money entices many to make foolish decisions. There are those who lay a guilt trip on people of wealth in order to get money from them.

So, what indeed is the value of obtaining much wealth? It will never satisfy the longing of the soul for peace and contentment. It will never deliver on its promise to make one happy. It can never fill the place of God in the heart. Only those who find their peace, contentment and joy in Christ will find true happiness. Only in Christ can one find a reason to live. Only in Christ does one discover how to deal with money in a way that both pleases the Lord and brings a sense of pleasure to the soul.

If you are driven by a desire for money, ask the Lord to change your heart's desire today to a desire for Him. Ask the Lord to help you put Him above all things. Ask Him to take His rightful place in your heart. Delight yourself in the Lord and you will find what you are searching for in life, both now and eternally.

MONEY CANNOT SATISFY

Eccl. 5:10-11 Those who have money will
never have enough. How absurd to think
that wealth brings true happiness! The more
you have, the more people come to help you
spend it. So what is the advantage of
wealth—except perhaps to watch it run
through your fingers!

There is not much that needs to be said
about these verses today. Much has been
written about money and our attachment to
it. The thought that I really think we need to
be reminded of is that if you have been
blessed with the earth's riches, it will never
satisfy your soul. No matter how much you
have, you will always want more. It is
ingrained in us because of our sinful nature.
We buy into the lie that enough wealth will
make us happy and satisfied with our lives.
We think that just a little more will do it.
We allow our lust for money to control and
drive us.

What we must get is that nothing can
satisfy the soul of man except a personal and

vibrant relationship with Christ. We are created to have a thirst for Him. There is nothing that can take the place of a relationship with Christ in your soul. He alone can bring you comfort, peace, joy, strength to keep on living, hope for tomorrow, a reason to live, and a reason to die. You will never find what your soul must have in life anywhere but in Jesus. The sooner we understand this truth, the sooner life will become worth the living.

One thing that is sure to happen if you are blessed with money is that there will be many who will be more than willing be there for you to help you spend it. It is built into our nature. Friends and family alike will want some of what you have. You will have an ingrained mistrust of people because of their greed. You will doubt the sincerity of those who express their loyalty and love to you. In turn, you will not be able to enjoy what you have like you would like to.

It is so easy to squander what wealth you have. Money easily flows through our fingers. Most of us will never have the luxury of having more than what we can spend. There is a great need for wisdom when it comes to wealth. We need to be good stewards of what the Lord blesses us with and not squander it away.

If your soul is not satisfied by Christ when you have little or nothing, it will never be satisfied when you have a lot. Seek the Lord and his righteousness and you will find everything the world promises you but cannot give you.

WEALTH FROM GOD

Eccl. 5:19 And it is a good thing to receive wealth from God and the good health to enjoy it. To enjoy your work and accept your lot in life—that is indeed a gift from God.

What is wealth from God? I believe it is far more than material wealth. It may include that, but not necessarily so. There are a multitude of believers who have never enjoyed the riches of earth and never will. Wealth from God is far more precious than the things of earth.

Wealth from God begins with a relationship with Him. It is knowing that our sins are forgiven, forgotten, and forsaken. It is living in peace with God and man. It is the wondrous gift of the Holy Spirit who actively works within us to keep us on a holy path to God. It is a hope that is certain, built on the promises of God himself. It is access to His Word and the understanding He gives us as we read it. It is the convicting work of the Holy Spirit

45

when we sin against God. It is God's mercy and grace. It is the fellowship of other believers to encourage us, teach us, and inspire us to a deeper walk with Him. Wealth from God is everything He provides for us to have eternal life.

Wealth from God does indeed often include the blessings of life on earth. We owe to God our resources for living, our health, our work, and our gifts to do the work He gives us to do. We are so blessed to be who we are and to do what we do. It should cause all of us to daily be grateful for our lives. We don't know how long our health will hold up and we don't know when changes will come in our lives that will drive us to our knees in despair; so we need to enjoy all that the Lord provides daily with thanksgiving and praise.

Most of us will face adversity in life. Things do not always go the way we want them to or the way they have gone before. The Lord sometimes withholds His blessings from us so that we will depend on

Him and not our blessings. Sometimes we have to lose what we have in order to appreciate God and what He gives. We grow the most in faith through adversity, not through affluence.

Dear friend, no matter what your circumstances may be today, accept it with gratitude before God. Fix your eyes upon the Lord and praise Him for His blessings. Learn what He is teaching you in this moment of your life. If you have much, use what you have to honor the Lord and serve Him. If you have little, trust Him for all that you need to see you through. He will supply all your needs as you walk by faith in Him.

ENJOY WHAT YOU HAVE

Eccl. 6:9 Enjoy what you have rather than desiring what you don't have. Just dreaming about nice things is meaningless; it is like chasing the wind.

Life would be so much easier and less complicated if we would learn this important lesson in life. We can eliminate most of the stress in living if we could learn to enjoy what we have in the moment instead of pining for what we don't have. Most people are simply not content with how their life is now and they long for more and better things that they don't have. Let's be honest about it. Isn't this why we spend so much of our lives working at jobs we mostly do not enjoy? We work so that we can get what we don't have so that we can have better lives than we have now. The sad thing of it is, usually when we get what we want we discover that it either is not what we really want or it does not give us the pleasure and satisfaction we thought it would.

The world runs on dreams. We are

constantly bombarded with things we don't have and think we might want. We think about those things and begin to develop plans on how to get them. Many are willing to see their dreams become a reality at any cost. Many will sell out their souls in order to pursue their dreams. What one does not have becomes far more important than one's relationship with God. Life is wasted away chasing after meaningless things.

A much better way to live life is to learn how to enjoy what you do have in the moment you are in. The only way we can do this is to learn to enjoy the presence of God in our lives. If we are not living in Christ, there is nothing in the world that will ever satisfy the soul. Life will be nothing but a meaningless chasing after that which will always disappoint us. Without Christ our dreams will defeat us. Only Jesus can bring us peace and contentment. Only Jesus can give life today and always meaning.

Don't put off enjoying life today in the pursuit of something that will not bring you lasting enjoyment once you obtain it. Live in the presence of Christ and each day will bring you pleasure as His grace unfolds in your life. Knowing that your soul is right with God alone can hold you steady in life regardless of the circumstances you are in. Each day, each moment, can be a blessing to be enjoyed when Christ is in it.

If you must dream, dream about the life Christ is preparing for you in heaven and live in preparation for that life. Life in Christ is the only life worth living for. It is the only life you can really find enjoyment in that lasts a lifetime.

TAKE PLEASURE IN CHRIST

Eccl. 6:9 Enjoy what you have rather than desiring what you don't have. Just dreaming about nice things is meaningless, it is like chasing the wind.

We are told constantly that what we have is not enough. We are bombarded daily with the promise that if we pursued a little bit more than what we have, we would be happy and satisfied. The thought is that more is better. There is a constant dissatisfaction that drives our lives.

We are reminded today that instead of always dreaming about what we don't have or letting ourselves be driven by the quest for more, we should learn to enjoy what we do have. Taking pleasure in what we have been blessed with and being content with it comes from deep within the soul. It would do us well to learn how to do it.

Taking pleasure in our situation in life comes from a heart of gratitude before God. The soul who is focused on the Lord and all that He brings to life is satisfied. Living in the richness of Christ's life is all that we really need. Experiencing the ever flowing living water of God's grace, living out daily the plan of God for life, being guided and empowered by the Holy Spirit, resting in the certainty of eternal life in Christ, and being transformed as we strive to live godly lives, are the most fulfilling and satisfy parts of living.

It is foolish to chase after those things which can never satisfy. It is foolish to waste our time and resources on those things which rob us of the joys of living. Blessed is he who knows those things which really satisfy and pursues them.

FUNERALS OR FESTIVALS?

Eccl. 7:2,4 It is better to spend your time at funerals than at festivals. For you are going to die and you should think about it while there is time. A wise person thinks much about death, while the fool thinks only about having a good time now.

At first glance, this verse may not make a lot of sense. Most of us would choose to go to a party than a funeral. Funerals are generally not a fun place to be. It is especially true if it is for someone who is very close to your heart.

Yet, when we think about it, we would have to admit that the value of a funeral to our souls far outweighs any good times we may have at parties. At funerals we are faced with the reality of our mortality. No matter how much we don't want to think about it, we are all going to die someday. When we die, there is no coming back and doing life over. We don't get a second chance to get it right. We don't get another chance to get ready to face God. We are vividly reminded of the fact that there are no guarantees as to how long we shall live. Death is but a breath away for us.

Wisdom tells us to think about these things. We still have hope as long as we have breath. The Lord has given us all the information and time we need to be ready to die. He waits patiently for us to take advantage of our opportunities, but when it is our time to die, there is no more patience. The Lord has determined how long we shall live and wise is he who understands this and doesn't wait until it is too late.

If you were to die today, would you be ready to face God?

YOU WILL DIE

Eccl. 7:2,4 It is better to spend your time at funerals than at festivals. For you are going to die and you should think about it while there is time. A wise person thinks much about death, while the fool thinks only about having a good time now.

Most of us would rather not spend a lot of time at funerals. Funerals are for people who we care about who have died. They are usually very difficult for us emotionally, especially if they are for people who have a very close tie to our hearts. We don't want to deal with losing someone we dearly love. We don't want to live life without those we love. We can't imagine what life is going to be like without them.

For some funerals are often a time of celebration for those whom we know are in heaven when they die, and they should be. However, it is also a time of grief as the reality sets in that they are gone, and it should be.

However, as painful emotionally as funerals are to us, they are a good thing. It is at funerals that we are most likely to think about our own mortality. God gives us the opportunity to examine our lives and make sure that we are ready to die. We need to periodically take a soul inventory. It is so easy to get so caught up into living that we ignore our dying. Each of us is going to die and we had better be ready at all times because no one knows when that moment will come.

Death is so unpredictable; it is but a breath away for all of us. We get this unfortunate notion that only sick or old people die. We choose not to consider that accidents happen all the time that take lives or that there are forces of nature that take lives. We ignore the fact that death can happen to us while we are enjoying life. It happens to other people, but not to us. But, it does happen to us. Only God knows when we will take our last breath. It is foolish to live life without death in view.

Living life to the fullest means that you are living your life in Christ so that you will be ready to die at any moment. It is not living in fear of death, but living in anticipation of that day when we will be with the Lord. Death is a good thing when we know that heaven awaits us. Is your living a testimony that you are ready to die?

FINISH WHAT YOU START

Eccl. 7:8 Finishing is better than starting. Patience is better than pride.

How many projects have you started but never finished? If you are like me, probably more than you care to think about. We have good intentions but often get distracted or discouraged and do not finish things we start. We may run out of resources before we finish what we are doing or run out of patience or the knowhow of how to proceed. Most people understand that failure to finish is a part of life. I admire those who know how to finish what they start and stick with it until it's done. I have to admit that it's not always the case with me.

It takes a lot of patience sometimes to finish a project you start. It's especially true of a big project. Sometimes the task is bigger than we can handle alone so we have to solicit the help of others. Most tasks take time as well as effort to complete.

When we start out walking with the

Lord, finishing is better than starting. So many start out well, better never finish. They may start out like a house on fire, but soon the flames die out and all that is left is ashes. So many get preoccupied with life and other interests and wander away from God. So many of us fail to establish spiritual disciplines early in our walk of faith and lose grip on what we had. We cannot ignore Bible reading, prayer and Christian fellowship and make it with the Lord. We cannot starve our souls of what they need and expect to keep on living. Life in Christ is a marathon, not a sprint. It's not how we start out that matters, it's how we finish.

Jesus told us to carefully count the cost of salvation before we start out because He knows how easy it is for us to get distracted, discouraged and defeated. Staying connected with the Lord does cost us a lot. It costs us our life goals and dreams. It costs us the hold the world has on us. It costs us giving Him control of everyone and everything in life that we hold dear. It costs us sometimes great suffering and even sometimes our lives. It costs us our selfishness and often a good standing with the world. Salvation requires of us great patience and perseverance as we journey through life.

Pride is one of our greatest enemies. It is so hard to not pat ourselves on the back for the things God has done in us and through us. It is something that we must constantly guard our souls against and whenever it rears its ugly head, we must surrender it to the Lord before it gets a foothold in us.

Don't be a quitter. Finish well what you have started. Live moment-by-moment in relationship with Christ and you will eternally be found in Him.

IN HIS FOOTSTEPS

Eccl. 7:13 Notice the way God does things, then fall into line. Don't fight the ways of God, for who can straighten out what he has made crooked?

Are you paying attention to the way God does things? Think about it. God lovingly works to draw all men to Him. He very clearly makes known the way to Him that we might walk in it. He makes a holy path for us to follow and demands that we walk on it. He aggressively sends forth workers into the harvest field of the world to reach the lost for Him. He equips His children so that they can effectively be witnesses for Him in the world. He warns us all about the consequences of sin and the reality of hell. He shows mercy and grace to all. He forgives all who sincerely repent of their sins.

We are commanded to fall in line with what the Lord is doing. We are to become like Him in His nature and actions. We are not to fight His ways but conform to them.

We are not to question His ways. The way in which we can do these things is to live in close communion to Him. It is not easy and you will face much opposition, but it is far better to struggle while following the Lord than it is to struggle because you are not following Him.

We must keep our souls in touch with God by spending quality time in His Word. There is no shortcut on this. It takes determination and discipline to stay in the Word and to learn from it. It takes time.

We must keep in touch with the Lord through prayer. There is no substitute for prayer. It is what we must do consistently and deliberately. It is an attitude we must live by. We must be a people of prayer.

When we feed our souls with the Word and spend time with the Lord in prayer, we must put feet to our faith and live it in the world. We must be witnesses of our faith both in deed and action. We must stop fighting against God and start living in cooperation with Him. There are not many ways to live life and make it to heaven. Jesus is the only way to God and we must walk in His footsteps wherever He would take us.

PAY ATTENTION AND LEARN

Eccl. 7:13 Notice the way God does things, then fall into line. Don't fight the ways of God, for who can straighten out what he has made crooked?

There are a couple of things we can do to discover how God does things. One thing we can do is to consistently spend time in the Word. There is great value in reading the history of God's dealings with man. Don't neglect the Old Testament record for we discover there much about God's holiness, mercy and grace. Before Jesus came God showed us through His dealings with man just how much we need a Savior.

In the New Testament we discover how much God loves us and how He solved our need for a Savior. Jesus came, lived a sinless life, went to the cross and died for our sins. In Christ, God showed us His love and holiness blended together into one. We discover that we don't have to be prisoners to our sins; Christ sets us free.

There is much about God that we don't know, but there is also much about Him we do know. We need to take note of how He moves amongst men and then fall in line. We discover quickly that when we get out of line, bad things happen. We get out of sorts with ourselves and the world around us. We become very weak and become easy prey to sinful temptations. We become defensive and often fight against God as He tries to gain control over us. We stumble around in the darkness and often cause ourselves much pain and suffering that could easily be avoided.

It is foolish to not follow the ways of the Lord. It is self-defeating and self-destructive. The only thing that is accomplished is making ourselves miserable. If you have fallen out of step with the Lord, don't take another step until you fall on bended knee before Him in repentance. There is great joy and peace in living in the Way. In Christ alone you will find what you are looking for and think you are finding on your own.

Notice how others are following the Lord. Follow the example of those who are living in Christ. If they can do it, you can too. There is a great cloud of witnesses God has provided for you to watch. Imitate their faith. And, be careful how you live because there are those who are watching you too.

WE ALL SIN

Eccl. 7:20 There is not a single person in all the earth who is always good and never sins.

This is a statement that is true for all people for all time. There is not one person who has ever lived, is now living, or shall ever live, who is so good he never sins. This includes you and me. No matter what others may think about you or what you may think about you, you are not as good as you may appear to be. Everyone sins and that is just a fact of life. It doesn't matter who you may be in the eyes of the world or church, you are guilty of sin. If you say you aren't, you are calling God a liar because He says you are.

Because we are guilty of sin, we need help from God if we are going to avoid the consequences of our sin, which is hell. God knew our plight and did what only He could do; He became human and lived a sinless life. He then took upon himself all of our sin penalty on the cross of Calvary when He died in our place. He who knew no sin became sin for us so we could have our sins forgiven by God. Not only did Jesus make it possible for God to forgive us, He made the way for God to forget we had ever sinned! When Jesus is our Savior, God does not look beyond the righteousness of Christ in us. It is as if we had never sinned!

Yes, we still sin because we are in the flesh and in the world. We are perfected in Christ but we are not perfect. Our sinful nature still haunts and harasses us. We are weak spiritually and will fail to measure up to God's holy perfection. But the Good News is that when we admit our sin and confess them to Christ, we are forgiven and our hearts are made whiter than snow before God.

In order to not live in sin and end up in hell, we need to stay closely connected with Christ. We must be washed clean by His righteousness. We must stay under His righteousness and not wander away from Him. He will protect us and keep us pure before God as long as we let Him be our

Savior and Lord. No one will ever be good enough to be with God without Him. No one.

NO ONE IS PERFECT

Eccl. 7:20 There is not a single person in all the earth who is always good and never sins.

Got it? You are a sinner just like the rest of us! No one on earth can make the claim that they are anything but a sinner in God's eyes. Some of us are sinners who are saved and kept by God's grace. We sin still, but we have God's help to overcome our sin.

Instead of God seeing us in all our sinfulness, He sees us as righteous and holy because He sees us through the filter of Christ's redemptive work on Calvary. For those who have not trusted Christ as their Savior, God sees them just as they are--- sinners without a filter. They stand before God on their own merit and are rejected by Him. They have no help or hope from God. They live in their sin and will have to stand before God with no one to be their advocate.

All of us need our Savior every day of our lives. We cannot handle our sin problem on our own. We need to constantly stay connected to Him through His Word, prayer, and the fellowship of His children. The more we allow Jesus to be our Lord, the less likely we are to sin. How close to Jesus are you living today?

LISTEN TO GOD

Eccl. 8: 1 How wonderful to be wise, to be able to analyze and interpret things. Wisdom lights up a person's face, softening its hardness.

Blessed is he who is able to read, meditate on, and understand the Word of God. Not everyone who reads or listens to the Word is wise. Many are unwilling to hear what the Spirit of God wants to say through the Word. We fail to grasp the mind of God because we often simply don't want to change our thinking or ways. God challenges us to a deeper walk with Him which requires much change in our ways. It is just easier for us to shut out the voice of God.

How wonderful indeed are those who come before God with open hearts and minds to hear and obey the Word of God. Wisdom is an absolute must for those who want to grow in their walk of faith. If you struggle with living out your faith in an honorable way before God, ask Him for wisdom. He will not withhold it from you.

Without wisdom, we are left to our own thinking about God. We filter God's Word through our sinful minds. We see things according to what we want to believe. We close our minds to the possibility that maybe we are wrong. We close our minds to the reality that we may be sinning against God. We often interpret things through the wisdom of man instead of God. We are led astray easily and often are guilty of leading others astray.

If you lack the wisdom to analyze and interpret things through the Spirit of Christ, take the time right now and ask the Lord to change you. Confess the foolishness of your ways and ask the Lord to forgive you for being so stubborn and self-sufficient. Ask Him to soften your heart so that you can hear His voice. Ask Him to give you a willing heart to let Him have His way in you.

Blessed is he who is able to read,

meditate on, and understand the Word of God. How wonderful it is to know that it is indeed the voice of God speaking to you and giving you understanding of the Word as you read it.

Take your time, tune in to God, and train your soul to hear God when He speaks to you.

WONDERFUL WISDOM

Eccl. 8: 1 How wonderful to be wise, to be able to analyze and interpret things. Wisdom lights up a person's face, softening its hardness.

Wisdom does not just happen or come naturally. It comes to those who live and learn. It is observing and applying to life what we learn so that we are better people than we were before. We learn from the mistakes others make and we learn from our own mistakes. Wisdom is making changes in our thinking and living as we discover newer and better ways to live. Wisdom comes to those who do not just "go with the flow" in life, but who deliberately strive to do those things which make them a better person. Wisdom gives a person confidence and a positive approach to living.

Wisest are those who are spiritually wise. It is a wonderful thing when God's children learn well how to live life in Christ. Those who are spiritually wise are students of God's Word. They do not just read the

Word for the sake of reading it, but they read it to learn about God and His ways. They read it with a desire to learn new things so that they can live more godly lives.

Those who are spiritually wise do not neglect their prayer time. They make it a point to spend time alone with God. They pray not only to be heard, but they pray to worship. They develop a mindset of praise and thanksgiving as they pray. They meditate on the awesomeness of God. They pray often just to have fellowship with God. They learn to enjoy being in the presence of God.

The spiritually wise do not neglect Christian fellowship. They learn to appreciate the faith of others and enjoy the fellowship of other believers. They learn that other like-minded believers are the best people on earth to know and fellowship with.

The spiritually wise are actively serving the Lord. They are those who have learned that it is far better to give than receive.

They grow to appreciate the opportunities the Lord gives them to do good amongst man. They seek to serve the Lord because they love Him and desire to honor and glorify Him. They have learned that there is no greater joy in life than to be ambassadors for Christ in the world.

Those who are spiritually wise are easily recognizable in the world. There is joy in their souls and it shows. They are known for their righteousness and compassion. They are gracious in how they deal with others. They are quick to forgive and slow to judge. They are a people after God's own heart.

A WORLD FULL OF EVIL

Eccl. 8:9 I have thought deeply about all that goes on here in the world, where people have the power to hurt each other.

We live in a time in which news about what is going on in the world is everywhere you turn. It's on our computers, TVs, radios, newspapers, etc. We may choose to ignore what is going on and pretend like it doesn't exist, but it does. Man's sinful nature is plastered everywhere. It is almost inconceivable how evil mankind can be. If we stop and think about it, it overpowers the soul.

Where will it all end? When will it all end? Is there anything we can do to stop the madness? How will this madness affect us personally if it continues? Is there any hope for our children/grandchildren if it continues as it is going? Is the way things are going in the world a sign that Jesus is coming soon?

Evil has always plagued the world. We

read history books and we read the Bible
and we are made aware of how bad evil is.
No matter how much people say that man is
inherently good, we know better. No matter
how much we like to think that life is better
today than it has ever been, it isn't. No
matter how much we try to bury the reality
of evil, it is everywhere and will continue to
plague man and only get worse.

The world is the present domain of
Satan. He is vigorously working to destroy
Christianity. He doesn't like children of
God and is determined to silence and
destroy us. God makes it very clear that
Satan is going to have his way on earth until
God puts an end to it. Jesus is coming soon
to take the Church out of the world so that
evil will manifest itself without restraint. It
is going to be a time in which God will rain
down judgment on the earth until Satan is
finally defeated and cast into hell for all of
eternity.

Jesus will take the Church out of the
world because He loves us and wants to

spare us the horrors of unbridled evil in the world. He loves us and gives us the means to be in the world but not victims of it. He takes up residence in the heart of all who repent and surrender their lives to Him and protects us from being destroyed by evil. We may have to live under the consequences of the world's evil, but we are not victims of it. In Christ we are the victors, the overcomers. In Christ, we are guaranteed to live with Him for all of eternity in heaven.

Do not let the news of the world overwhelm or overpower you. Live faithfully in Christ and you will live in peace and have joy in your soul, no matter how bad things may get around you.

PUNISHING CRIME

Eccl. 8:11 When a crime is not punished, people feel it is safe to do wrong.

Have you ever noticed how some people seem to always get themselves into trouble? We often wonder why they keep doing it. The answer is simple; doing the crime is worth the time when the cost of doing the crime is not severe enough to make one want to stop it. People do not fear punishment when it is not sufficient to deter crime. When a person is basically slapped on the wrist for their wrongdoing, they will continue to do what seems right in their own eyes regardless if it is a crime or not. I know that when growing up if I behaved wrongly, I was painfully disciplined for it. I learned very early in life that the pain for the crime was not worth doing the crime.

We see the result every day of a soft attitude about crime. Parents ignore what their children do, people don't tell on those they know are doing wrong, pastors overlook sin in the church, people in the church overlook their pastor's sin, people in authority are allowed to do whatever they want with little consequences, etc. We reap what we sow and we should not be surprised at the result. The heart is wicked to the core and people will do evil much more easily than they will do good. When crime is not punished, people will feel safe to continue doing evil.

The Lord disciplines us so that we will learn what not to do in our walk with Him. He knows that only a holy heart will be able to make it into heaven. He loves us and does all He can do to help us to keep our hearts holy. He quickly points out our sins and holds us accountable to Him for them. He loves us and refuses to let us feel safe in continuing in our sin. He knows that He who sins will be held accountable before God for them and He longs to spare us from our own folly.

Do not get mad at God when He holds you accountable for sin and disciplines you. He does it because He loves you and desires a relationship with you. Instead, be thankful. Thank the Lord that He is merciful as well as just. Thank Him that He loves you and cares about your soul. Thank Him for not leaving you alone to die in your sin. Thank Him that He provides a way out of your sin. Thank Him that He does not hold your sin against you once He forgives you. Thank Him that He does not look beyond the righteousness of Christ in you and that your past sins are no more in His sight. Thank Him that He is on your side and will always strive to help you to be holy before Him.

GOD'S GOOD LAW

Eccl. 8:11 When a crime is not punished, people feel it is safe to do wrong.

Law exists to control the tendency to sin against God and others. Without law, there is nothing but chaos. Everyone will do whatever their sinful desires want to do, regardless of how it may affect others. The message of the law is that damaging or destructive behavior has consequences. Law exists to protect those who do right from those who don't.

When the law is not enforced, people learn that they can continue bad behavior and get away with it. We are born sinners and therefore sin will be our natural tendency. Unenforced law is very damaging to the soul and will ultimately lead to self-destruction.

God gave us His law to reveal our sinful tendencies. He makes it very clear that we are our own worst enemies when left to ourselves. It is impossible for us to be good on our own. The Lord clearly shows us at our worst and compares us to himself. We quickly find out that we need help if we are ever going to be able to do what is right before God. The Law is very clear, sin is punished by God. Man cannot get away with sin.

We need the Law to remind us of sinful behavior and attitudes. We need to understand how guilty we are before God. We need to understand that bad choices result in bad consequences. When we choose to sin against God, there is a price to pay.

We need to thank the Lord for showing us just how far short we are of His holiness. Thank the Lord for showing us our need for His saving grace. Thank Him for daily reminding us how to live in holiness. Thank Him for not letting us get away with sin. Thank Him that He gives us the means to overcome our sin. Thank Him for His righteousness and holiness in us so that we might not sin against God.

DO YOUR BEST

Eccl. 9:10 Whatever you do, do well. For when you go to the grave, there will be no work or planning or knowledge or wisdom.

There is no second doing of life. You only get one chance to get it right. You cannot press a reverse button and do it all over again. If you mess up you have to live with the consequences of what you have done. Therefore, strive to get things right the first time. Do your best to live a life of honor before God and man. Do what God has given you to do while you can do it. Don't mess around and half-heartedly serve the Lord. Give Him your best effort. You will die with the consequences of how you have lived. While you have the time and energy to do something about it, give of your best to the Master. Don't put off another day what you know God wants you to do. Today is the day of opportunity, tomorrow may never come.

What are you doing with your life? Are you doing your best to honor Christ with it?

Don't be like the majority who settle for mediocrity in their lives. Do your best to be the best you can be for that is what pleases God. How you live is a reflection of your true feelings about Christ in you. He deserves nothing but the best of you, not the leftovers.

Remember, God will reject those who are lukewarm followers of Him.

STAY SHARP

Eccl. 10:10 Since a dull ax requires great strength, sharpen the blade. That's the value of wisdom; it helps you succeed.

It is just good sense to make the best use of the equipment we have. We want to maximize the usefulness of what we have. It is so much easier to use equipment that is at its best than to try and use equipment that is in poor shape due to neglectful care. We can spare ourselves a lot of stress and effort by using only equipment that is in good condition.

Wisdom tells us the same thing is true of our souls. When we take good care of our souls, we are able to maximize life and what it brings to us. There is great living to be lived but it is only found by those who live rightly before God. The Lord doesn't want us to live mediocre lives. He wants us to enjoy the best of what He has to give to us. He wants us to know His peace and the fullness of His life. He wants us to live in victory and not defeat. He wants for us joyfulness in our salvation. He withholds those things from us, however, when we don't take care of our souls.

We will never know the better life until we consistently pursue God. In order to keep our souls sharp, we must be into the Word of God. We must explore its riches by reading and meditating on it. We must have open hearts as we read it so that the Lord can have His way with us. We keep ourselves sharp by consistently staying connected with the Lord in prayer. We talk and listen as we wait before Him. We speak tenderly to Him and worship Him as our God. We stay sharp by consistently living for Him in all we do. We let Him be an influence in our lives in all things.

Successful living in Christ is guaranteed to all who keep their souls in good working order.

SEEK WISDOM

Eccl. 10:10 Since a dull ax requires great strength, sharpen the blade. That's the value of seeking wisdom; it helps you succeed.

Wisdom helps us to succeed. In fact, without wisdom we will not succeed. Wisdom is the ability to take what we know and make good use of it in our lives so that we become better people. It requires humility and the willingness to make changes in our behavior and thinking when it is necessary. Wisdom is learning to work on our weaknesses and to shore up our strengths. It is gained on the foundation of dedicated work.

Spiritual wisdom doesn't just happen because we have faith. It comes to those who are fully surrendered to the Lord. The Spirit of Christ gives wisdom to those who are serious about their walk with the Lord. It requires from us a committed and consistent study of God's Word. It requires of us a commitment to worshiping the Lord. It requires of us letting the Lord govern our

90

daily living.

Wisdom is the acknowledgement that all that is good comes from God. It is recognizing the work of God in all of life and in us. It is not taking for granted the handiwork of God. It is being grateful for the blessings of God. It is not blaming God when things don't go our way. It is submitting to God's authority over us with no strings attached. It is not being satisfied with the status quo but always seeking to grow in grace and knowledge. Wisdom is stressing those things that help build us up in faith and staying away from those things which tear us down. Wisdom is resisting Satan whenever he endeavors to entice us away from God and into sin.

The key to successful living in Christ is to seek wisdom. We need to have an insatiable desire for the Lord and for understanding on how to live holy lives. Wisdom is the solid rock upon which faith is built. Wisdom is found only in Jesus who is our Solid Rock.

GENEROUS GIVING

Eccl. 11:1 Give generously, for your gifts will return to you later.

Are you a giver? How do you treat the things God has given you? Do you let them go reluctantly, dutifully, or gratefully? Do you consider the opportunity to give a privilege and honor, or is it a drudgery to you? How you view giving is a good indicator of what is in your heart.

No matter what the Lord has given to you, you are but a steward of it. The Lord has put His confidence in you to use your gift wisely and generously for His honor and glory. He believes in your capability of being a good steward. Whether you have little or much, the truth is the same. You are to give generously to the Lord with a willing heart. What you give can be a lot of different things: money, time, energy, talents, wisdom, encouragements, hospitality, etc. You have something the Lord has given to you to use for His glory. He has entrusted you with the responsibility of nurturing and growing your gift so that you can give it generously back to Him to be used for His service.

What gift(s) has the Lord given to you? What are you doing with it? Are you hoarding it or generously giving it for the glory of Christ? Generous giving can only come from a loving heart and hoarding comes from a selfish heart. Is your heart right with God? If so, let your life show it by being a generous giver

ACCOUNTABLE TO GOD

Eccl. 11:9 Young man, it's wonderful to be young! Enjoy every minute of it. Do everything you want to do; take it all in. But remember that you must give an account to God for everything you do.

No matter what stage of life you are in, remember this sobering truth: you must give an account to God for everything you do. It is true of everyone. We are responsible for the way we choose to live. If you are not living a life rooted in Christ, you will be held responsible for it by God. There is no one who will get away with anything before God.

If you are a Christian, you are held to a higher standard than those who do not profess Christ. It is serious business to proclaim Jesus as your Savior and then not live like it. Jesus is the holiness of God personified. God will not be mocked by the way we live. We are to live in the righteousness and holiness of Christ, which means we strive to not sin. We do our best to protect the honor of Christ by living lives worthy of His name. We desire to please Him in all we do. Taking the name of Christ as our own is not to be done lightly. It matters a great deal to God and He holds us responsible for what we do.

Are you living a life worthy of the name of Jesus? If not, you need to repent right now and with Christ's help, start living a godly life. You will give an account to God for everything you do.

LIFE PREPARATION

Eccl. 12:1 Don't let the excitement of youth cause you to forget your Creator. Honor him in your youth before you grow old and no longer enjoy living.

Now that I am in the "older" stage of life, I certainly can see the wisdom of this verse. When we are younger we seldom see the need to establish habits of life that will sustain us when we grow older. In youthful energy we plow ahead with reckless abandonment, striving to get the most out of the moment. We put off until another day the things we know we should be doing for tomorrow. We live as if we will always be in the youthful stage of our lives. But, we do grow older and before we even realize it, our days of opportunity slip away.

We look back upon our lives and often wish that we had not been so foolish. We regret choices we made and life patterns we have established. We begin to realize that life would have been so much different and better had we listened to the counsel of those who had already walked the walk.

It is especially true of our spiritual lives. It is in our youth that we are most likely to turn to the Lord. It is in our youth that we are most likely to establish godly habits that will sustain us and enable us to grow in grace and knowledge of the Lord. It is never too late, but it is a lot harder to draw near to the Lord in our later stages of life than it is in our youth.

Regardless of what stage of life you are in today, seek the Lord now while you can. You can't reclaim missed opportunities, but you can do something about what is your life now. Don't let another day or moment go by before you seek the Lord. You will be glad you did.

FEAR AND OBEY GOD

Eccl. 12:13,14 Here is my final
conclusion: Fear God and obey his
commands, for this is the duty of every
person. God will judge us for everything we
do, including every secret thing, whether
good or bad.

Solomon had looked at life. He
observed how futile life really is. He sought
meaning and purpose for our existence
through our life experiences and came up
empty-handed. When he was all done
looking, he came to the conclusion that in
order for life to have any meaning at all, it
must be rooted in our relationship with God.

Solomon is widely known for his
wisdom. In his day people from all over the
world came to listen to him. He recorded
his thoughts and God preserved them for all
the generations to follow. We continue to
benefit from his wisdom as we strive to live
the life of faith. He was very observant
about life and faith. So, when he narrows

done all that he understood about life into a couple of sentences, it is wise for us to take note.

Solomon declares that the most important thing we can do in life is to fear God and obey His commands. Fear involves respect. We must respect God in His holiness. We must always be mindful of the character and nature of God. Our awareness of God compels us to obey Him. We obey Him because we know the character of God and realize that whatever God tells us to do it is because He loves us and desires to make us holy. He declares that without holiness no one will see Him, let alone be with Him. Wisdom would teach us that we must have proper respect for God in His holiness.

The Lord does not want us to face Him without being holy in character. He knows that on Judgment Day everything in our hearts will be exposed for Him to see and if we are not holy, we must spend eternity in hell. He will see every secret thing. He will see all the goodness of our hearts and all the evil. He will know not only what is there but why it is there. He will know our motives and whether or not we strive to live in Christ or not. He will know if we live for Christ out of duty or love. Nothing will be hidden from Him.

There is nothing more important in life than this: to fear God and obey Him.

LIVING IN CHRIST

Eccl. 12:13,14 Here is my final conclusion: Fear God and obey his commands, for this is the duty of every person. God will judge us for everything we do, including every secret thing, whether good or bad.

Solomon had spent a lot of time thinking about life and its meaning. He had the opportunity and resources to look into just about everything that is common to man. He looked for purpose and meaning in what man does in life, and came up empty time and time again. He discovered that there is no lasting purpose or satisfaction in anything people did with their lives.

At the end of his search, Solomon turned his thoughts to the eternal. He declared that what really life was all about was to fear God and obey Him. He declared that it is the duty of every person to do it. Much has been declared about what it means to fear God.

To fear God is to have a deep respect

for who God is in His holiness and what He does for those who sin against Him. It is having a healthy sense of God's judgment. It is living with the knowledge that God hates sin and will not tolerate it in His presence. It is respecting the reality of hell as a place of eternal tormenting suffering for those who reject Christ and live in sin. It is understanding that we are not able to draw near to God because of our sin. A healthy fear of God drives us to Christ who alone can make us holy before God.

We don't like to think about it much, but God will judge us for everything we do. Every hidden thing we have done, good or bad, will be exposed before Him. God sees what no one else sees. He knows all that we do and even why we do it. We don't like to think about it. God knows everything we do or think about, good or bad. No one always thinks about good things or always does good things. All of us are guilty of sin. No matter how hard we try, we can't get away from God's knowing eye. Such knowledge should cause us to fear what awaits us when we face God.

Only those who are living in Christ will be able to stand before God. Jesus is our holiness, our righteousness before God. He is the only one who can keep us from being subject to the wrath of God. God will bring wrath upon all in whom He finds sin. When sin is exposed it will be dealt with. Hell has been prepared for those in whom sin is found. When God looks at the soul who is living in Christ, He sees not sin; He sees the righteousness of Christ. He will never look beyond the righteousness of Christ. Thus, for those who live in Christ, our sins are as if they never were. Our only hope is to fear God and obey Him, which means we live in Christ and let Him be our Savior and Lord.

DON'T LOOK DOWN ON ME

Song of Songs 1:6a "Don't look down on me, you fair city girls, just because my complexion is so dark.."

We do it, don't we? We look down on others who are different than we are. We know better, but we struggle with not doing it. For some reason we profile a person based on their appearances. We shy away from those who look different and maybe even shun them.

I am reminded of what God told Samuel when he was looking for the one God was going to raise up to replace Saul as king. Samuel knew that the next king was going to be from Jesse's family. He assumed it would be the oldest son, but it wasn't. One by one a son of Jesse was brought before Samuel and God told him that it wasn't him. After looking at seven sons of Jesse, Samuel asked if that was all of his sons because by this time Samuel was confused since none of the sons were chosen by God. Finally, the youngest son, David, was brought before Samuel and God told him he was the one.

God told Samuel that he wasn't seeing what He saw. Man looks on the outside and passes judgment; God looks on the inside and passes judgment.

Many friendships are lost and many qualified people are passed over simply because they look different. Shame on us!! Don't be so quick to dismiss someone because of how they may look. Take the time and put forth the effort to get to know the person's heart. Ask the Lord for discernment in the process and you will perhaps discover someone very special in your life, someone who will prove to be a true-blue friend for life.

THE OBJECT OF ONE'S LOVE

Song of Songs 2:1 "I am the rose of Sharon, the lily of the valley."

One of the "Goldie oldie's" of church hymnals is, The Lily of the Valley. I also remember as a kid singing about the sweet Rose of Sharon. Both songs speak of Christ, the Lord of life. The songwriters express praise to our God for Jesus. Jesus is lifted up far above all else. He is the exalted one, the King of Kings and Lord of Lords. "He is the bright and morning star, the fairest of ten thousand to our souls." It is always good to focus our eyes on the Lord and appreciate who He is to our souls.

Just like this young woman was declaring that she was the object of her lover's heart, Jesus is the object of our hearts of love. She was zeroed in on her lover (Solomon). All that she could think about was him. She longed to be with him and throughout this book of love, we discover how beautiful love can really be.

So it should be with us with Jesus.

Are you in love with Jesus? Do you long to be near Him? Does He set your soul on fire? Do you do whatever you can do to be with Him? If you are like most, probably not. Why? What has happened to draw you away from the Lord? What has taken away your desire to be near Him, to be bathed in His love?

Whatever it is, why not change what is and return to your first love? Ask the Lord to give you a love bath. Ask Him to wash away the grime and dirt so that you can feel fresh and pure once again. Reset your priorities and make Jesus your life. Reacquaint yourself with Him. Look for Him in His Word and in your prayer closet. Don't make excuses; just do it. You have the time for what really matters to you. Only Jesus is worthy of being number one in your life.

UNTIL THE TIME IS RIGHT

Song of Songs 3:5 "Promise me, O women of Jerusalem, by the swift gazelles and the deer of the wild, not to awaken love until the time is right."

The world has no restraints on "love." Most people do not care about waiting for marriage to express their physical desires for someone. Most people let their passions dictate their behavior. The idea of self-control before marriage is deemed to be unnecessary, unrealistic, and even unacceptable by many. We live in a very physically orientated world.

Yet, God clearly sets boundaries for our moral behavior. He tells us that intimacy should be reserved for marriage. He declares that sex outside of the context of the marriage of a man and woman is sin. God created us with our passions for the mutual benefit and enjoyment of a married couple for life. Sex seals the covenant of love between a husband and wife and makes them as one in God's eyes.

Wise are those who do not "awaken love until the time is right." Wise are those who care enough about each other that they set clear moral boundaries that they will not cross to help minimize their passions. Wise is the couple who strive to keep themselves pure by avoiding those things and situations that would arouse them. Wise is the couple who keep their eyes fixed on Jesus so that He can help them keep their passions under control until the time is right.

There is no greater expression of love than intimacy in marriage. When done within marriage and within the boundaries of God's moral laws, there is no guilt, shame or regrets with sex. Don't rob yourself of the best of what God has for you by tarnishing it and yourself before marriage.

EXCLUSIVE LOVE

Song of Songs 4:12 "You are like a private garden, my treasure, my bride! You are like a spring that no one else can drink from, a fountain of my own.

Even though he didn't always practice it, Solomon understood the concept of exclusive love within marriage. For a married couple, one's spouse is the only object of his affections. There is a commitment to one's spouse that excludes anyone else from their relationship.

Marriage is a covenant relationship between a husband and his wife before God. There are gates put up where no one can pass through. There is no one else allowed in their hearts or marriage. A husband is exclusively his wife's and his wife is exclusively his. No one else is allowed to get close enough to be a threat to their marriage.

When a couple sees their relationship as being exclusive, there is no looking on the other side of the fence and pining for someone else. There is no entertaining and feasting on the attention of others. There is no reason for mistrust to rear its ugly head. There is no insecurity during those times when intimacy does not happen.

When God created man and woman and brought them together and they became one, He knew exactly what He was doing; He knew that it was exactly what both the man and woman needed in order to live life at its best. What a wonderful gift of love marriage is from our Heavenly Father. Don't mess it up. Love your spouse exclusively and only let your spouse be the one who loves you.

AUTHOR'S PAGE

The Lord moves in mysterious ways. I have been involved in church ministry as a pastor for over 40 years of my life. I have served mainly as a bi-vocational pastor with virtually no thought given to being an author. But, the Lord had other ideas.

I had my first book published in 2009, C Through Marriage. I continued writing, but did not pursue any further publishing while still active in my ministry.

The Lord changed my agenda since my retirement from the ministry. He led me into a writing ministry that blossomed online. I did a lot of personal devotional writings which I poste online.

Due to unforeseeable circumstances, my publisher went out of business. When that happened, I learned how to self-publish through Amazon's Create Space and now have several books on the market that deal with marriage and daily devotionals. You will find them listed on my author's page at https://goo.gl/KoHuQL.